From the scrapbook of

**HOPE FRELENG SHAW and
SYBIL FRELENG BERGMAN**

As if growing up with the man who drew Bugs Bunny and being the models for Tweety (petite and blonde!) weren't joy enough, our father, Friz Freleng, went on to create the Pink Panther, just as we entered adulthood and could appreciate the shift from cute to cool.

Within weeks of his debut, the Pink Panther was on the cover of Time magazine, and shortly there-after, Pink Panther shorts began earning top honors, including an Academy Award. Dad and David DePatie created hundreds of short films that continue to generate giggles the world over to this day.

Dad always credited the Pink Panther's success to his silence. Rarely did he speak, other than with expressions (and mischief) recognized around the globe. And yes, he might have gotten one or two ideas about mischief from us!

Your paw print here

MEET...

...THE **PINK**

PANTHER™

HOPE FRELENG SHAW
and SYBIL FRELENG BERGMAN

Illustrated by
ART LEONARDI

UNIVERSE

First published in the United States of America in 2005

by

UNIVERSE PUBLISHING

A Division of Rizzoli International Publications, Inc.

300 Park Avenue South · New York, NY 10010 · www.rizzoliusa.com

Text by Hope Freleng Shaw and Sybil Freleng Bergman

Illustrations by Art Leonardi

2005 2006 2007 2008 2009 / 10 9 8 7 6 5 4 3 2 1

Printed in the United States of America

ISBN: 0-7893-1308-1

Library of Congress Catalog Control Number: 2005925695

Design by Headcase Design

This book is dedicated to

Henry, Skyler, Sam, Caroline, Lily, Alexander, Benjamin, Adriana, Christopher, Dustin, Caila, Heather, Adam, Nicholas, Heidi,

and all those who came after the creators of the Pink Panther.

Be cool. If you watch and listen carefully, there's a lot to laugh about in life!

Do you recognize that cat?

That's the Pink Panther. The Pink Panther.

Now, you might have seen him around, but do you know his story? No? Well, allow me . . .

Many years ago, there was this really,
really big diamond.

It was found way down deep underground.

Every once in a while, diamonds have flaws—
tiny spots that reflect light differently than
the rest of the diamond.

This particular big diamond had a flaw in it that looked like a leaping panther–a pink panther–and so it was named the Pink Panther Diamond.

Each person who owned the diamond would
look closely at it to find the flaw.
He or she would stare right at the flaw, never suspecting
the Pink Panther was a real pink panther.

One day, someone thought the diamond was so unique,
he gave it to his king. The king in turn decided to give it
to his young daughter as a gift for her to keep
and wear for her eighteenth birthday celebration.

After trying on the diamond, the king's daughter
carefully locked it away in a safe. It was a dark, lonely,
boring place, but there it stayed for days and days
until the big event. Meanwhile, word of this priceless
and rare diamond spread throughout the kingdom.
It was coveted by many thieves.

When the princess's eighteenth birthday arrived,
she opened the safe to retrieve the diamond. But before she
could get it, a thief sneaked in and grabbed it.

This theft gave the Pink Panther the chance to
jump out of the diamond and split!

Not to worry. He made a purrfect landing on his feet,
as any cat would.

The Pink Panther was just about to
sneak out of the palace when he heard the king
order a police inspector to find the diamond.

Though he didn't seem very clever,
he introduced himself as Inspector Clouseau,
one of the world's greatest detectives.

Inspector Clouseau went on and on about
his honors in his native France.

The Inspector was especially proud of his attention to the finest details.

The Pink Panther realized that if this
Inspector Clouseau was as good as he claimed,
the world would soon know his secret.

They would learn that the "flaw" had disappeared
from the famous diamond, and that the Pink Panther
was in fact real and on the loose!

If Inspector Clouseau found the diamond
and discovered that the Pink Panther was gone,
the Inspector would be forced to find him
and return him to the diamond.

The Pink Panther hated the idea of going back into the diamond, and ultimately back into that dark safe. When that boastful Inspector Clouseau vowed to find the diamond, the Pink Panther resolved to get to it first!

Inspector Clouseau immediately declared
that Paris was the most obvious place to start
looking for the stolen diamond. Any self-respecting
jewel thief would take his prize there to sell.
The Pink Panther followed close behind.

While on the plane to Paris, the Pink Panther thought about the disguises he would need so that he could follow Inspector Clouseau without being noticed.

So, to blend in while tailing the Inspector,
the Pink Panther took on many an odd job.

There was a rumor that the thief might try to take the diamond to England.

The Pink Panther immediately got a job
as a train conductor on the Eurostar,
the train that runs through the underwater tunnel
between France and England.
But he overslept and missed the train!

Luckily, Inspector Clouseau's England lead
was a false alarm.

While the Pink Panther waited for Inspector Clouseau's
next move to find the diamond, he got a job dressing
mannequins in a department store.

The department store was a
great source of disguises!

It was also an especially good hiding place.
For a while.

Now the Pink Panther and Inspector Clouseau
would be tracking each other!

At the department store, the Pink Panther got his next big tip. He overheard some models talking about how one of them would get to wear the diamond in a fashion show!

The Pink Panther called in a favor
and got a pass to be a photographer at the show
to keep an eye on things. Enjoyable as the show was,
there was no sign of the diamond.

While he continued casing Inspector Clouseau
and the diamond, the Pink Panther decided to work
for the famous Louvre art museum.

On a day off he met an artist trying to sell his work.
It wasn't very good.

Back at the Louvre, the Pink Panther tried to give the poor fellow some painting tips. After all, his museum experience should count for something!

The painter didn't seem very pleased.

Exasperated and feeling underappreciated,
the Pink Panther decided his next job
would be outdoors.

The Pink Panther went to the countryside to be
a nature photographer. The wildlife was breathtaking.
And it felt wonderful to get away for a while—
not another soul for miles!

Hearing that the Pink Panther Diamond might have been spotted in Versailles, the Pink Panther headed for a small artists' colony outside the palace.

Sharing space with a "mysterious" comrade in art,
the Pink Panther passed the days with no sign
of the thief or the diamond.

Soon the Pink Panther's artmate up and left.
The Pink Panther had a hunch that this
"painter" would eventually lead him to the diamond.
He quickly followed him to London.

To pass the time,
the Pink Panther joined the London Philharmonic.

At first the Pink Panther played the violin.
But he was the only one who seemed to know the right music.
He ended up playing several different instruments,
and eventually conducting!

On second thought, being in the spotlight might not
have been the best idea.

The Pink Panther gave the Inspector the slip
and headed for the good old U.S.A.

As luck would have it, a job opened up.
The Pink Panther tried his hand as a reporter for
the Daily Blabbermouth.

Wouldn't you know, his first assignment was to interview ...
INSPECTOR CLOUSEAU! The editor had gotten wind that the
Inspector was in the country on a case.

What a perfect opportunity to find out
what Inspector Clouseau was up to!

His story on Inspector Clouseau made the front page.

After that huge break, the Pink Panther was
put on the Hollywood beat. Among his first interviews was
a big-shot director. They got to chatting
about the Pink Panther's many adventures and all
his assumed identities.

Quelle surprise! It wasn't long before the Pink Panther became a movie star.

Of all places, his first location shoot
was back in Paris!

After starring in a few movies, the Pink Panther couldn't walk down the street without being mobbed for photos and autographs.

He made the cover of magazines.

He even had a balloon for a parade made in his honor.
However, after a few years, living in the limelight
grew tiresome.

Meanwhile, Inspector Clouseau needed to think.
Where was the diamond? Happening upon an abandoned house,
he spied the perfect place to sit and mull things over.

Satisfied with his many lives—certainly more than nine!—
the Pink Panther wasn't too upset when Inspector Clouseau
actually found the diamond.

Even if it meant returning to live in it.

Mission accomplished, Inspector Clouseau
bought an "abandoned house" and retired
to the country in his native France.

Case closed.

To Holly Shaw for her tireless enthusiasm and
creativity in helping us introduce another generation to the Pink Panther.

To Lisa Leonardi-Knight for her assistance in inking and painting the illustrations.

To Pamela Cannon and Jane Newman for their patience
and perseverance in making this book a reality.

To David DePatie for helping realize Hope and Sybil's father's dream of artistic autonomy.
We are grateful that David and Friz came to meet as they did, and that together
with Blake Edwards, they conjured that magic formula to integrate vision and trust,
talent and savvy, to create such a universally loved character as the Pink Panther.

And last but not least, to Elaine Piechowski and the MGM team for their support.